PM Traditi
Tales and Plays
TEACHERS' GUIDE

Gold Level

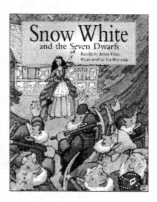

MANDI RATHBONE &
MICHELE GORDON

NELSON PRICE MILBURN

Contents

About the PM Library

Story Books, Traditional Tales and Plays, and Animal Facts

The basic philosophy

'Children learn best with books that have meaning and are rewarding' ... *Reading in Junior Classes*, New Zealand Department of Education.

'I can read this!' All books in the PM Library are **centred on meaning**, but they are also designed to give children the rewarding experience of **success**. If a child can read one book they should be able to read another and another. Success should follow success. When the right match of 'child to book' is made, the greater the child's interest and the greater his or her desire to read.

On every page in every book care is taken with the sentence structures, the choice of words, the clear well-spaced type, and with the meaningful, accurate illustrations. Because the books are easy as well as interesting, children are able to practise a variety of reading skills and enjoy the feedback of success. They learn new words — and practise them again and again — all the time understanding what they are reading about, and returning to the books with pleasure *because* they have real meaning, and emotional impact.

The criticism levelled at many 'stories' written for beginners is that most are not stories — they are highly repetitive reading exercises in which meaning comes a poor second. Teachers and children have often been disappointed by the bland banality of most early school 'readers', with pages that were shaped not by a story-teller but by a need to repeat known words, or sentence structures or letter clusters, as often as possible. In revulsion from these interest-starved, over-repetitive non-literary exercises, some modern teachers have built their reading programs around library picture books that are worth reading for their own sake — only to discover that too many children are defeated when presented with 200 or so basic words in quick succession. It is not easy for average beginners to sort out *were was with will well would who why what when where which went want won't walk watch wall wait work wash warm word* ... it never will be!

The authors of the PM Library have worked hard to combine the virtues of two approaches — **controlled basic vocabulary** to let children master a growing number of common but confusing high frequency words,

and **storytelling** quality to engage the mind and emotions and make learning to read satisfying. The authors have been well supported by a team of highly talented illustrators.

Features of the PM Story Books

The books have many ingredients, and all stories are rigorously considered and shaped to meet high standards.

All stories have:
- *meaningful content*. The situations and concepts can be understood by young children. The resolution in each story is logical — these stories encourage children to think by *letting* them think. The books are full of opportunities for intelligent discussion and logical prediction.
- *well-shaped plots*. Tension appears early in each story — something goes amiss — and the problem is solved by the end. It is tension that keeps children and teachers interested in the story — what will happen next? When the problem is finally resolved the ending is satisfying.
- *no sexism, racism or stereotyping of people*. Some women have supportive roles but others work — there is a female police officer and a female engineer. Jack's dad is a caregiver. Black, Asian and Caucasian children all have a turn at being central characters. The books include a boy with Down's syndrome, and a girl and a boy who both use a wheelchair. The elderly, too, are shown leading active lives.
- *a wide spread of subjects* to meet the different experiences and enthusiasms of as many children as possible.
- *warmth and emotional sensitivity*. The child heroes are successful problem solvers — they are never laughed at, and never made to look inadequate. Animals are treated with sensitivity, too.
- *language that is satisfying to the ear*. The rhythms of good English — storyteller's English — are there. These stories pass the test of good literature and they sound satisfying when they are read aloud. The power of these stories is enhanced by balanced phrasing, and the right word in the right place.
- *considerable scientific accuracy*. Because accuracy matters, the dinosaur stories are carefully written to

reflect recent research, and Toby the tow truck solves his towing problems in technically accurate ways. All stories are checked for accuracy.

- *well-designed typography*. At this level a serifed type-face gives words coherence and individuality. The spacing of words, lines and paragraphs enhances readability. The classic typeface has been selected for its exceptional readability.
- *elisions*. These continue to be consolidated.
- *a rate of new word introduction strictly held to 1 in 20*. When each new word is supported by at least 19 known words the decoding process is easier. Children are reading well away from *frustration level*. They are at a success level where reading is enjoyed. They are reading for pleasure and meaning. By the end of Gold Level, children will have mastered more than 600 high frequency (heavy duty) words as well as many *interest* words. It is reassuring to know that these high frequency words account for about 80% of the words used in most passages of narrative English written for adults.
- *many opportunities to learn about the way words work*. At this stage of their reading children have to be able to turn written letters into spoken sounds, continue the sounds and check the message. The reading process depends on all three skills. When faced with a new word, children need to be shown how to break it into syllables or letter clusters. Successful decoders have to be flexible and have enough confidence to keep trying. Confidence is built from past successes, from application of syntactic and semantic cues, and from mastery of words and letter clusters met before. Through experience, children will become aware that the vowel *a* is likely to represent one of five sounds: *a* as in *at*, or *ah*, or *ape* or *all*, or *ago*. In English it is flexibility that leads to successful decoding.
- *attractive well-drawn illustrations* that enable children to gain maximum understanding as they match picture with text, and vice versa. Meticulous care has been taken with these hard-working pictures. These are books that children will return to again and again with delight.

Features of the PM Traditional Tales and Plays

- *Although these stories are simplified short versions of the well-known tales, a great deal of the original flavour has been kept.* Most of the tales have been firmly anchored in time and place so that *The Three Billy Goats Gruff* is clearly Norwegian, *Stone Soup* reflects the poverty of the time in which it was written and *Rumpelstiltskin* is a true representation of the superstition that pervaded 14th century life in much of Europe.

- *Each part in each play* is colour coded to lessen confusion and help children understand the conventions of a printed play.

Features of PM Animal Facts

- *Vocabulary is linked to the grading of the Story Books and Traditional Tales and Plays*. The grading logo, a coloured petal, indicates the recommended level for Guided Reading. As with the Story Books and Traditional Tales and Plays, the introduction of each new word is supported by 19 known words.
- *Non-fiction has a different 'dialect'*. Many sentences are short, and the necessary introduction of new interest words (mostly nouns) is accompanied by exact picture clues. Children reading non-fiction have to learn to link photographs and text and 'read' them together, as both inform. Each paragraph stands alone. Children do not have to hold the thread of a story in their minds as they read — pages can sometimes be read out of order, and the book approached through its index. All these things (short sentences, abundance of picture clues, absence of a developing plot) mean that many children find non-fiction less demanding than fiction, and even more enjoyable.
- *Non-fiction has a standard layout*, with new components that can be explored in PM Animal Facts, e.g. contents page, clear headings, labelled diagrams, alphabetical index.
- *A linear self-correcting program*. The questions at the foot of the page are not designed to make children research other books, nor to 'trick' them. Their purpose is to build confidence and to secure information. The immediate re-reading of a page of text to find or check an answer leads to careful thought, and greater retention of knowledge.
- *PM non-fiction books have reliable information*. Thorough research and scientific accuracy matter in all books in the PM Library, not least in the non-fiction books.
- *High interest levels*. In spite of their simplicity, these books arouse interest, e.g. Did you know that ... birds evolved from dinosaurs? ... skunks do a special dance before they go hunting? ... goldfish can be black? ... guinea pigs are called cavies? ... some cats like vegetables? Even adults will learn something new.
- *Independent research*. The simplicity of the text and the clarity of the layout allows young children to taste the delights of independent discovery.
- *Links with the PM Story Books* increase children's understanding, adding depth to both strands. Many PM Story Books are supported by non-fiction titles: *Nelson the Baby Elephant* is matched with *Elephants* (PM Animal Facts: Animals in the Wild); *Owls in the Garden* is matched with *Owls* (PM Animal Facts: Nocturnal Animals).

Using this Teachers' Guide

Before beginning the PM books at Gold Level, children will have read the PM books at the Orange, Turquoise and Purple levels. They will have acquired more than 550 high frequency words and many other interest words. These books will have allowed the child to develop confidence, skills and independence, and to think critically about language and meaning. Predictability and logic are an essential part of these stories. It is this strong focus on logic and sense that helps children form the habit of self-correction. **Meaning** is the most important element in all PM books.

The Teachers' Guides have been designed to assist busy teachers to plan and develop challenging language opportunities in their classrooms. The PM books should be used with a wide variety of other books and materials to ensure that children succeed at each level before they proceed to the next. The ideas described in each Teachers' Guide can be adapted for other books.

There are Teachers' Guides for each colour level.

The large daisy logo has eight coloured petals showing the more advanced levels that follow the familiar 12 of the daisy 'clock'. The eight are: Orange 1, Orange 2; Turquoise 3, Turquoise 4; Purple 5, Purple 6; Gold 7, Gold 8.

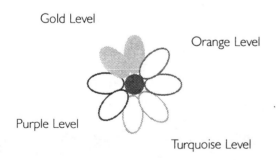

Gold Level

Orange Level

Purple Level

Turquoise Level

By the end of Gold Level, children should have reading ages of 8+ years.

Each Teachers' Guide has suggestions and ideas for guidance in the use of the PM books at that level.

Emphasis has been placed upon the development of the language skills — speaking, listening, reading, writing, viewing and presenting. These skills are common to all curriculum areas. Reading is not treated as a subject that stands alone.

Creating the atmosphere

This is the 'tuning in' stage. It is the time when the teacher focuses the children's thinking on the content or concepts of the tale. At this stage, related language or exciting new vocabulary can be discussed, written on the whiteboard or sometimes acted out. In this way, new ideas become familiar and the children's language is enriched.

Focusing on the tale

Guided reading

Book study is an in-depth study of the tale. It is a time to follow the plot, to become emotionally involved in the tension, the climax and above all to enjoy — perhaps predict — the satisfying ending.

It should be such an enjoyable experience that the children will want to read the tale right through to the end all by themselves. Because new high frequency words have been introduced slowly and carefully in the tales, children can achieve this success.

Going beyond the tale

Teachers may select from or adapt these language enrichment activities to suit the needs of their own classes. Some activities are suitable for small groups of children to work at together, others are for individuals. Some may even be taken with a whole class. All have been designed to develop purposeful stimulating language. They give children ample opportunity to interact verbally, not only with teachers but also with one another. Some activities in mathematics have been included to extend children's thinking and experiences beyond the tale content. The art and drama activities will allow children opportunities to express themselves and help them to make sense of their reading.

Books to share and compare

These are suggested titles of books by other authors and from a variety of publishers. Children need to have many stories read to them, often. They soon know that reading is enjoyable and will want to return to favourite books to read themselves. Occasional questions about the stories will sharpen the focus, prompt interest and talk, and ensure that children listen with understanding.

Reading aloud to children is one of the best ways of enriching their vocabulary and increasing their general knowledge.

Blackline masters

Blackline masters of mask templates for most characters in the plays have been included in this Teachers' Guide. Making masks will provide children with opportunities for:

- reading and following instructions
- co-operative problem solving
- mathematical discussion about proportion
- individual creativity.

It is recommended that the templates be photocopied onto lightweight card. A headband to secure the mask can be made from a 3 cm strip of card long enough to fit around the child's head. Secure the strip of card to each side of the mask.

Plays

The plays can be read by children with the reading and analytical skills required at Gold Level; the structures and words used are those that they can read with confidence. Each play should also be able to be read with understanding because the tale which the play is based on has just been read in guided reading (it is easier for children to act out a familiar story). In addition, the plays can also be read by young children who are looking at a play script for the first time. The coloured panels, which indicate particular characters, let the children know when their parts appear.

The tales and plays at **Gold Level**

The number of fishermen in this tale fluctuates with the various tellings — sometimes six, seven or twelve. Hence the tale has been called *The Twelve Men of Gotham.* The conceptual difficulty of remembering to count oneself is timeless.

Setting: England (Gotham is near Nottingham)

Era: circa 1800

Ensure that the children have a variety of models of this type of writing to follow.

Seven Foolish Fishermen

Creating the atmosphere

- Sing the song 'One Man Went to Fish' featured on the inside front cover of the book.
- Discuss different types of fishing, e.g. rod and reel, fly fishing, nets. Talk about the equipment required.

Focusing on the tale — guided reading

- Study the cover illustration and read the title. Have the children predict why the seven fishermen are called 'foolish'.
- pp.2–5 — Read the text together. Talk about the different places the seven fishermen chose to fish. Emphasise the prepositions used.
- pp.6–7 — Discuss why Tom wanted to count the fishermen.
- pp.8–9 — Point out Matt's position in relation to the other six fishermen. Why was this important as he counted the others?
- pp.10–11 — The fishermen are counted again and again. Discuss why the word *foolish,* in the title, is important.
- pp.12–13 — Ask, 'Why are the fishermen looking around frantically? What do you think will happen?'
- pp.14–19 — Read the text and examine the illustration carefully. Talk about Robin's role in the story. Ask, 'Do you think Robin knew what the problem was before he counted the fishermen? Is Robin clever or foolish?' Have the children provide reasons for their answers.
- p.20 — Discuss why the men are happy. Ask, 'Do you think they are still foolish? Why?'

Going beyond the tale

- Have the children reread pp.2–5. Invite them to draw the river scene and each fisherman fishing at his correct location. Encourage them to write a brief description beside each fisherman, e.g. 'This is Matt fishing from the right bank.'
- Have a class discussion on the dangers and the positive aspects of rivers. Following the discussion, brainstorm all the words associated with rivers and list these on the whiteboard. In groups have the children make a word find featuring the words listed. Groups could then swap and complete each other's word finds.
- Revise the meaning of the word *retold.* In pairs have the children retell another PM Story Book or Traditional Tale as an illustrated comic strip with the dialogue in speech bubbles.

- Have the children discuss the importance of a river to a community — both in traditional and modern-day societies. Encourage them to consider things people can do to protect a river for future generations, e.g. correct disposal of rubbish and other wastes, limited fishing.
- Make a large class mural showing a local river and its wider environment. Add labels derived from the previous activity's discussion.

- Invite the children to gather five fishing related poems. Have them re-key the poems on the computer using various kinds of type and design, or they could handwrite each poem in an attractive way. Ensure that the titles are not present. The children can then glue the poems into a booklet and provide each poem with a new title. Introduce the concept of a contents page and have the children write a contents page for their booklet. Encourage them to design a cover and write a title for their booklet, e.g. 'Fishy Poems'.
- In groups have the children make a magnetic fishing game. Provide paper, sticks, string, magnets and paper clips. The game could involve fishing for a joke, fishing for an instruction or fishing for a word to be put into a 'silly' sentence. Have the children decide upon and write the rules of the game. They could then teach the game to a junior class.

> Provide opportunities for the children to search for information in a variety of texts.

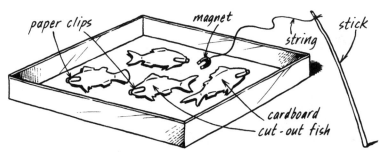

- Have the children work in pairs, designing and then constructing a bridge out of cardboard. Prior to this activity, provide pictures of various kinds of bridges. Talk about their structure and the types of material used in construction. Once each pair has made their own bridge, discuss who made the strongest (test the bridges by recording how many wooden blocks each will hold), what part of the bridge needs to be the strongest and what is holding each pair's bridge up.
- Look closely at pp.14–15. Pay particular attention to the hats worn by the characters in the tale. Compare and contrast the similarities and differences. Have the children design and make a suitable fishing hat. Encourage them to think about wind, sun, glare, rain, etc.
- Have available a selection of pictures and reference books on river fish and sea fish. In groups have the children research two or three fish from either group. Encourage them to choose an original way of presenting their information to the class, e.g. poster, concertina booklet, using overhead projector transparencies, mural.

Books to share and compare

- *The Fisherman and His Wife,*
  Margot Zonach,
  Blackie Publishers, 1969.
- *Seven Blind Mice,*
  Ed Young,
  Philomel Books, 1988.
- *The King's Commissioners,*
  Arleen Friedman,
  Scholastic Inc., 1994.

This story has been adapted from *The Bee, the Harp, the Mouse and the Bum-Clock* (*Donegal Fairy Stories*, Sedmas McManus, Doubleday, 1990). It contains strong echoes of *Jack and the Beanstalk*, and of Grimm's *Simpleton and the Golden Goose* (in which a king's daughter could not laugh). The kingdom, the castle and the magic harp give a medieval flavour to this cheerful Irish story.

Setting: West Ireland

Era: 15th century

Jack and the Magic Harp

Creating the atmosphere

- Write the word *harp* on the whiteboard. Ask the children to share what they know about harps. Discuss their ideas in detail.

Focusing on the tale — guided reading

- Read the title. Look closely at the illustration. Notice the thatched cottage, surrounding farmland and the characters' clothing. Discuss when and where the tale is set.
- pp.2–3 — Examine the illustration of the village fair. Ensure that all the children understand the significance of a fair in a country village, i.e. buying, selling and exchanging wares.
- pp.4–7 — Ask, 'What was Jack supposed to do with the cow at the village fair? What did he do instead? Why did everyone dance when the bee played the harp? Do you think the harp was magic?'
- pp.8–13 — Discuss how Jack is sent back to the market to sell two more cows but again he swaps them.
- pp.14–15 — Ask, 'Why was Jack's mother furious? What news does the neighbour have for Jack? How might this help their unhappy situation?'
- pp.16–17 — Have the children predict how Jack will make the princess laugh. Identify the court jester in the illustration and discuss his costume.
- pp.18–19 — Read the text with the children. Have them summarise the three things that made the princess laugh. Were the children's predictions correct?
- p.20 — Ask the children why Jack's mother no longer thinks he is foolish.

Going beyond the tale

- Jack succeeded in making the princess laugh three times. Invite the children to list three original ideas that they would carry out in order to make the princess laugh.
- Have the children design a poster proclaiming the king's plan to make his daughter laugh. Encourage the children to think about the information required, the need for an eye-catching design and layout, and the appropriate lettering and sentence structure for that era (some research may be needed). Make the poster look authentic by smudging it with ash or coffee and rolling it into a scroll.

- Provide folk dance music appropriate to the era. In groups of four, have the children make up a suitable dance to accompany the music. Encourage the children to teach the dance to other groups of four.
- Read a version of *Jack and the Beanstalk*. Compare and contrast this story with *Jack and the Magic Harp*. Compile a large Venn diagram showing the similarities and differences between the two stories.

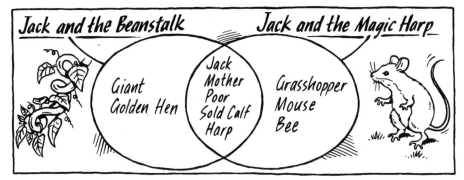

Help the children to think critically and discuss information.

- Look closely at the cottages on p.4. Have the children make models of these, complete with thatching. Construct them out of boxes, straw, card, pebbles, ice-cream sticks, and stones. Display the cottages together to form a class village.
- Have the children choose either the bee or the grasshopper in the story and draw a detailed sketch. Encourage them to research their chosen insect in reference books, label its body parts and write a brief summary describing its characteristics.
- Examine the illustration of the court jester on p.17. Discuss the role of a court jester in a royal palace hundreds of years ago. Invite the children to think of three riddles, tricks, games or songs and to present them to the class. Share one or two performances a day. Encourage the children to design and make a court jester's costume for the performers to wear.
- Look closely at the illustrations on pp.2–3, 6–7 and 10–11. Talk about the stalls featured and the goods bought, sold and swapped. Encourage the children to find illustrations of other similar market scenes in reference books found in the library. In pairs have the children choose one stall and have them make a collage or paint a large picture of it. Display all the stalls together on a class mural depicting a market scene.

- Look closely at the illustration of the magic harp on the title page and p.12. Have the children design and make a harp. Make available a range of construction materials, e.g. wire, string, rubber bands, bamboo, sticks, card, boxes, nylon, etc. Extend this activity and allow the children to make a different instrument, e.g. guitar, drum, flute, chimes. Hold a simple concert for another class.

Books to share and compare

- *Jim and the Beanstalk,*
  Raymond Briggs,
  Puffin, 1973.
- *Jack and the Meanstalk,*
  Brian and Rebecca Wildsmith,
  Oxford University Press, 1994.
- *The Miller, the Boy and the Donkey,*
  Brian Wildsmith,
  Oxford University Press, 1969.
- *Jack and the Animals,*
  Donald Davis,
  August House, 1995.

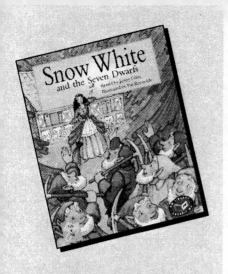

The best-known version of *Snow White* is the one collected by the Brothers Grimm (published 1823). Until 1848, Germany was divided into many small kingdoms, giving rise to countless tales of royalty. An older semi-magical belief, also included in *Snow White*, was that dwarfs mined gold and silver in remote mountains.

Setting: a German kingdom

Era: circa 1700

Snow White and the Seven Dwarfs

Creating the atmosphere

- Talk about the word *dwarfs*. Discuss other small mythical characters often featured in traditional tales, e.g. elves — *The Elves and the Shoemaker* (PM Traditional Tales and Plays Turquoise Level), leprechauns — *Patrick and the Leprechaun* (PM Story Books Gold Level).

Focusing on the tale — guided reading

- Read the title with the children. Look at the cover illustration. Ask, 'What do you think the seven dwarfs do for a living?' Have the children justify their answers. Examine the title page illustration. Ask the children why a basket of apples is featured and why one is by itself.
- pp.2–3 — Read the text and chant the verse in italics. Look closely at the illustration and discuss the vanity of the new queen and the opulent surroundings.
- pp.4–5 — Read the text and chant the new verse in italics. The mirror's response has changed. Why is the queen furious? How does she attempt to solve her problem?
- pp.6–7 — Have the children count the following items — beds, pillows, blankets, chairs, spoons, plates and cups. Take particular note of the size of these items. Ask, 'Who lives here? Why aren't they home?'
- pp.8–9 — The dwarfs are very surprised to see Snow White. Discuss the situation and how the dwarfs and Snow White would be feeling.
- pp.10–11 — Why does the Purple Dwarf warn Snow White not to answer the door to anyone?
- pp.12–13 — Read the text and chant the verse. Discuss the wicked queen's plan.
- pp.14–15 — Is Snow White really dead or just in a deep sleep? Look closely at the facial expressions of the dwarfs and discuss how they must be feeling.
- pp.16–17 — Why was the prince fascinated with Snow White?
- pp.18–20 — Read the text with the children. Discuss how the tale ends for Snow White, the prince, the dwarfs and the queen.

Going beyond the tale

- Every morning the dwarfs went off to work down in the mines and returned home in the evening. In pairs have the children write a possible timetable showing a typical dwarf's working day.

6.00 am	Get up and wash	4.00 pm	Bring coal up from
7.00 am	Eat breakfast		underground
8.00 am	Off to work	5.00 pm	Home again
9.00 am	Digging down in the mine	7.00 pm	Dinner
12.00 noon	Lunch	8.00 pm	Read and sleep
1.00 pm	Loading coal onto trolleys		

- Have available a variety of apples for the children to taste. Encourage them to suggest words which accurately describe the characteristics of an apple based on the children's five senses (taste, touch, smell, sight, sound). Use the language generated from this activity to write poems on apple-shaped paper.

Apples
Crunchy, sweet and smooth,
Delicious apples,
Yum, yum, yum!
Round and shiny,
Green or red,
Apples so very juicy.

Provide opportunities for children to write in different text forms.

- Search through the tale and list the seven colours associated with the dwarfs. In groups have the children mix various shades of each colour, e.g. light orange, dark orange, yellow-orange, etc. Invite them to paint the various shades of the seven colours onto a circular piece of cardboard to represent a colour wheel. Labels could be added.
- Have each child bring a favourite apple recipe from home. Compile these into a classroom 'Apple Recipe Book'. Trial some of the simpler recipes.
- Ask the children to draw half of the wicked queen's face as shown in the diagram. Have them hold it up to a mirror to see the image reflected. Try the same activity using the face of another character in the tale, e.g. a dwarf, the prince. As an extension to this activity, have the children exchange their picture halves with a partner. The partner can then complete each picture. Share the new images and display them in an interesting way.

- Have the children make their own mirror by smoothing a large piece of tin foil over a thick piece of card. The children could also design and create interesting frames to surround their mirror using sea shells, corks, pressed flowers, straws, etc. Spray paint the frames with metallic paint.

Books to share and compare

- *Snow White in New York,*
  Fiona Franch,
  Oxford University Press, 1986.
- *Oh Snow White,*
  Hawksley Gerald,
  Koala Books, 1998.
- *Snow White and the Red Rose,*
  Brothers Grimm,
  Hamish Hamilton, 1998.

In England, *Rumpelstiltskin* was called *Tom Tit Tot*; in Scotland, *Whuppity Scoorie*; in France, *Ricdin Ricdon*; and there are Scandinavian tellings, also. *Rumpelstiltskin* was collected by the Brothers Grimm in the early 1800s, but the story is much older. It preserves the ancient superstition that supernatural power can be broken if a secret name is known — in many primitive societies identity, name and power are intertwined.

Setting: Northern Europe

Era: circa 1300

Active participation in a group encourages the children to reflect on their own ideas and gather information from others.

Rumpelstiltskin

Creating the atmosphere

- Show the children a picture of a spinning wheel. Discuss how, in the past, spinning wheels were used to make fabric for clothing. If possible, look at natural raw wool and a ball of spun wool.

Focusing on the tale — guided reading

- Read the title with the children. On the whiteboard write *Rumpelstiltskin*. Break the word into syllables. Have the children identify as many 'small' words as they can.
- pp.2–3 — Ensure that the children know the meaning of the word *boasting*. Examine the illustration. Ask, 'Where is the miller and his daughter?' Talk about the importance of the village market square in times gone by, both as a place to sell wares and a place of general gossip. Notice the king's palace high on the hill. Ask the children how the king may have heard about the miller's daughter.
- pp.4–5 — Discuss what the king is demanding of the miller's daughter. Why is she sobbing?
- pp.6–13 — A strange little man comes to the rescue of the miller's daughter. What does she give him in return? Discuss the greed of the king and why he wishes to marry the miller's daughter.
- pp.14–15 — Discuss the consequences of the promise the miller's daughter has made to the strange little man.
- pp.16–17 — Why has the strange little man reappeared? What does he want? Discuss the expression on the queen's face. How might the queen go about finding out the strange little man's name?
- pp.18–19 — Read the text. Ensure that the children appreciate the tension created on p.18. Have the children predict what will happen.
- p.20 — Discuss the ending to the tale and the queen's stroke of luck enabling her to outsmart the strange little man.

Going beyond the tale

- Have the children reread the chant 'Rumpelstiltskin is my name so fine, tomorrow the baby will be mine.' In pairs have them write two more verses to complete the song. Invite the children to make up a dance to go with their verse and to share both with the class.
- Invite the children to design a poster offering a reward to anyone who can discover the strange little man's name.
- Have a class discussion on how Rumpelstiltskin may have felt about the events in the story. Re-write the tale as if Rumpelstiltskin had told it. Display the children's work as a wall story. Invite them to add matching illustrations.

- Talk about things that are made of gold, in particular those seen in the story, e.g. ring, crown, throne. With the children, make jewellery out of salt dough. When the item is cooked and cooled, spray it with gold paint.

Salt Dough Recipe
2 cups of flour
½ cup of salt
1 small cup of water
Mix the ingredients with your hands until a ball of dough is formed.
Roll and shape the dough into the required shapes. Put them on a greased baking tray and bake for two hours at 180°C.

- Talk to the children about the meaning of the word *boast*. Have the children sit in pairs and encourage them to boast about things they are good at doing. Follow with a class discussion on why some people boast.
- Invite a spinner or weaver to demonstrate their craft to the class. Prior to the visit, have the children prepare suitable questions to ask.
- Look closely at the illustrations in this book and notice the buildings of the era. Invite the children to look through reference books for further details. Using cardboard, boxes, glue, paper, etc. have them construct detailed models of similar types of buildings.
- Revisit the tale and notice the clothing worn by the various characters. Examine, in particular, the head-gear worn by the women on pp.14–15. Compare these with the head coverings worn by the peasant women on pp.2–3. Examine the men's clothing and their hair styles. Talk about the similarities and differences to the clothing we wear today, e.g. we also wear leggings and tunic-style tops. Invite the children to make one of the head coverings featured in the tale out of scrap material, stockings, cardboard, etc. Encourage the children to parade their head coverings for other classes to view.

Use role play to communicate ideas.

Books to share and compare

- *Politically Correct Bedtime Stories,*
  James Garner,
  MacMillan Publishing Company,
  1994.
- *The Classic Fairy Tales,*
  Iona and Peter Opie,
  Oxford University Press, 1974.
- *The Little People: A Book of Fairies, Elves and Dwarves,*
  John Patience,
  Derrydale, 1990.

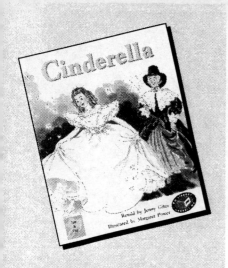

Perrault's tale is the best-known of all the Cinderella-type stories and was published in 1697. Iona and Peter Opie (*The Classic Fairytales*, Oxford University Press, 1974) describe hundreds of tellings in many languages, including a thousand-year-old Chinese version with remarkable parallels to the current telling. In earlier centuries, a girl's only chance of moving from rags to riches was by making a fortunate marriage. *Cinderella*, the all-time favourite fairytale, epitomises this romantic dream.

Setting: any small European princedom

Era: 19th century

Cinderella

Creating the atmosphere

- Write the words *traditional tales* on a chart. Discuss the meaning of these words and ask the children to recall other traditional tales that they have read. List some of the titles and have the children orally summarise and share each tale's basic story line.
- Reinforce the meaning of the word *retold*. Discuss how some details can change when a tale is retold orally and over many years. Point out, however, that the main story line usually remains the same.

Focusing on the tale — guided reading

- Discuss the cover and title page illustrations. Identify the characters and the items. Notice the clothing worn and discuss the possible setting and era.
- pp.2–3 — Examine the illustration and identify the four characters. Pay particular attention to their clothing, body language and body positions. Discuss possible reasons why Cinderella is feeling sad and lonely.
- pp.4–5 — Look at the facial expressions of the stepmother and the ugly sisters. How are they feeling and why do they want to go to the Grand Ball?
- pp.6–7 — Discuss Cinderella's unhappiness and why she, too, would love to go the ball.
- pp.8–11 — Talk about the splendid carriage, horses and gown, and Cinderella's astonishment at their appearance. Summarise the changes the Fairy Godmother made by performing her magic. Ask, 'What is the one thing Cinderella must remember?'
- pp.12–13 — Discuss the illustration and appreciate the grandeur of the occasion. Ask, 'How would Cinderella be feeling?'
- pp.14–15 — Examine the illustration and discuss the time on the clock tower and why Cinderella has disappeared so suddenly. Have the children predict what the prince will do.
- pp.16–17 — Ask, 'Why are the ugly sisters fighting over the slipper? Why is it so important that it fits them?'
- pp.18–20 — The shoe fits Cinderella. The prince has found his princess. Enjoy the happy conclusion to the tale.

Going beyond the tale

- Look at four different types of footwear, e.g. football boots, dancing shoes, work boots and sneakers. Have the children choose one of these pairs of shoes and pretend they can talk and feel. List and then discuss the following points on the whiteboard: what the shoes might say to the people who wear them, things that might happen to the shoes, places the shoes might go and complaints the shoes might have. Invite the children to write and then illustrate a story about the life of the shoes they chose.

- Talk about the information that usually goes on an invitation. Have the children write and design two invitations — one for a 'Great Ball' and one for a disco at their school. As a class, share, compare and discuss the differences between the two types of invitations.
- Have the children design and make their own magic wands. Ask them to then write about three everyday items they would like to transform. They should say what they would transform them into and why.
- Talk about Cinderella before and after her transformation. Discuss the differences. Have the children draw 'before' and 'after' portraits of Cinderella. Encourage them to write appropriate adjectives around each illustration.

- Talk with the children about formal attire worn to balls in Cinderella's day, e.g. suits, top hats and tails, ball gowns, bonnets and shawls. Have a class ball. Recreate the atmosphere by having the children decorate the classroom appropriately and wear home-made costumes.
- Invite the children to design a ball gown or suit and bow tie appropriate to the era of the tale. Have them add accessories of their choice. Invite the children to label their designs and display them in the classroom.

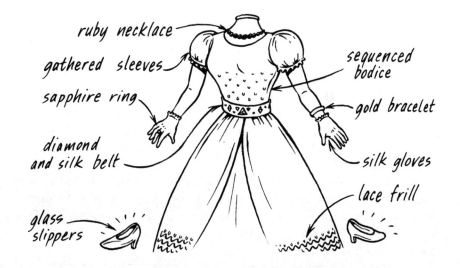

Books to share and compare

- *The Real Cinderella Rap,*
  Alan Trussell-Cullen,
  Nelson ITP, 1994.
- *Cinderella and the Hot Air Balloon,*
  Ann Jungman,
  Frances Lincoln Ltd, 1992.
- *The Cinderella Show,*
  Janet and Allan Ahlberg,
  Viking Kestrel, 1986.

- Record the play (see pp.21–31 of the story) onto audio tape. Encourage the children to use expressive voices appropriate to each character, e.g. Cinderella — a quieter and more gentle voice, the ugly sisters — loud and harsh voices.

The most familiar telling of *Beauty and the Beast* stems from a French version published in 1756. The 'message' that handsome looks are less important than a caring nature makes it more satisfying than many of the romantic traditional tales. *Beauty and the Beast* is a very old story of enchantment and virtue rewarded. The Roman legend of Cupid and Psyche has strong parallels.

Setting: Italy

Era: circa 1400

Encourage the children to contribute to discussion respecting the views of others.

Beauty and the Beast

Creating the atmosphere

- Write the words *Beauty* and *Beast* on the whiteboard. List a variety of words that the children associate with these terms, e.g. Beauty — *pretty, graceful, beautiful, sweet, kind*; Beast — *scary, ugly, monster, frightening*.

Focusing on the tale — guided reading

- Read the title with the children. Discuss the setting and the woman's style of clothing. Have the children predict the significance of the rose on the title page.
- pp.2–3 — Read the text. Why is the merchant so unhappy? How does Beauty react to his news? What about her sisters? Discuss the opulent nature of the family's clothing and surroundings. Predict what their life will be like in the country.
- pp.4–5 — Ask, 'What do you think will happen to the merchant?'
- pp.6–7 — Discuss the beautiful surroundings. Ask the children who they think lives in the castle and why they have not appeared.
- pp.8–9 — The merchant picks a rose for his daughter. What is the consequence of his action?
- pp.10–11 — Discuss Beauty's bravery and the selfishness of her sisters.
- pp.12–13 — In what way did the beast show his true kind nature? What does he ask in return for his kindness? How does Beauty react?
- pp.14–15 — Discuss Beauty's reasons for leaving the beast. Ask, 'Why does the beast say he will die if she does not return? Why does the beast give Beauty the magic ring?'
- pp.16–17 — Compare the family's surroundings to those on pp.2–3. Ask, 'Why are Beauty's sisters jealous of her?' Recall what will happen to the beast now that Beauty has broken her promise.
- pp.18–19 — Who is the handsome prince?
- p.20 — Discuss the reason why the beast changed back into his original form.

Going beyond the tale

- Reread *Beauty and the Beast* to the children. As a group, develop a character study of the beast. Encourage the children to think beyond the text as they suggest words to describe his personality and physical appearance. Now have the children choose one other main character from another traditional tale. Invite them to draw a picture of this character, and list words to describe his or her personality and physical appearance.
- Look at the food on the table on p.6. Talk about the possible contents of each dish (use a variety of reference books featuring common foods of the era). In pairs have the children write an appropriate menu for the merchant's dinner and a menu for a present-day dinner. Compare and contrast the two menus.

~ Merchant's Dinner ~
Entrée ~ Duck liver pâté
          Turnip soup
Main ~ Roast lamb
Dessert ~ Wild berries

~ Tonight's Dinner ~
Entrée ~ Chicken Soup
Main ~ Sausages and potato
Dessert ~ Ice-cream

- With the children, revisit the tale in order to find verbs that give strong images, e.g. *growled, snarled, roared*. List these words and others that the children can think of on a classroom reference chart. Discuss how some words describe an emotion more vividly than others, e.g. *said* can be replaced by *roared*. Encourage the children to refer to the listed words when writing stories of their own.
- In small groups have the children retell the tale in their own words using a felt board and cut-out felt characters, or an overhead projector and cardboard silhouettes of the characters.
- Collect a variety of roses from bud to full bloom. Have the children look closely at them and talk about the characteristics of each stage of a rose. Divide a sheet of paper into three sections and have the children do an observational drawing of a rose at each stage.

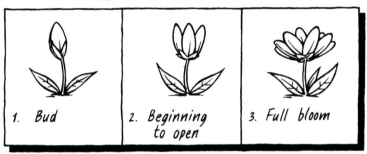

1. Bud   2. Beginning to open   3. Full bloom

- Arrange a visit to a local theatre company to view costumes similar to those depicted in this tale. Discuss these in detail. Some children might like to follow up the visit with some observational drawing.
- Have the children create a three-dimensional castle from boxes, card, cylinders, cellophane, etc. Look closely at the illustrations on pp.8 and 18. Point out details such as turrets, shingles, windows, flags, fortress, spires, height.

Books to share and compare

- *The Beauty Who Would Not Spin*,
  Adele Fasick,
  Scholastic, 1989.
- *The Ugly Duckling*,
  PM Traditional Tales and Plays
  Turquoise Level,
  Annette Smith,
  Nelson ITP, 1998.
- *The Frog Prince*,
  Adapted by Lucy Kincaid,
  Brimax Books, 1981.

- Have the children reread the text and list words that describe the feelings apparent in the tale, e.g. *jealousy, anger, kindness, bravery, fear*, etc. In groups invite individuals to dramatise one of these emotions while the other children guess which one it is. Allow each child a turn to act out an emotion.

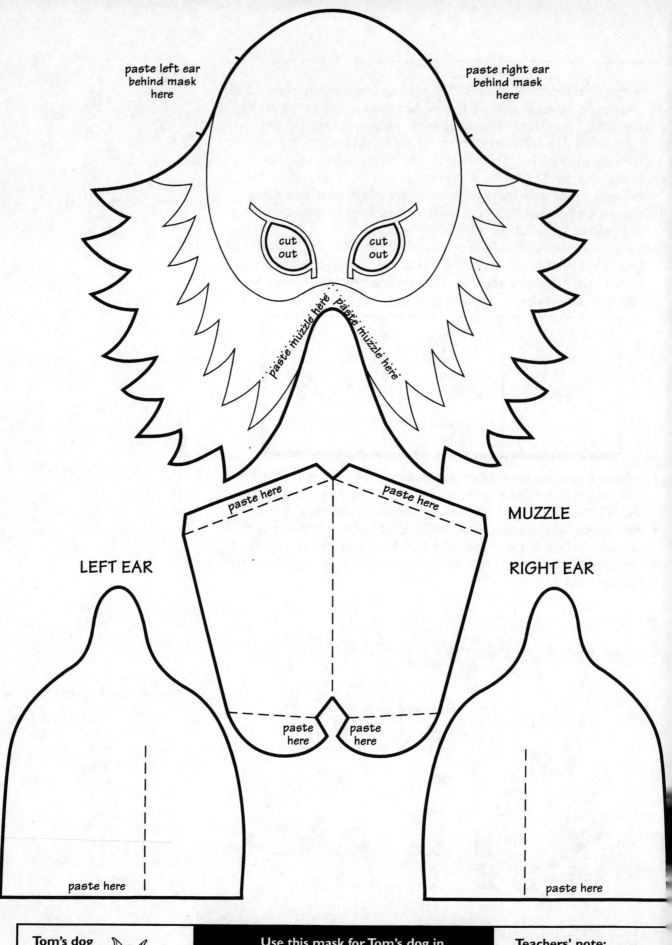

paste left ear
behind mask
here

paste right ear
behind mask
here

cut out

cut out

paste muzzle here   paste muzzle here

paste here   paste here

MUZZLE

LEFT EAR

RIGHT EAR

paste here   paste here

paste here   paste here

Tom's dog 	Use this mask for Tom's dog in *Seven Foolish Fishermen* **Colour and decorate the mask.**	Teachers' note: **Enlarge this template 150%**

PM Traditional Tales and Plays Teachers' Guide Gold Level (Set D)

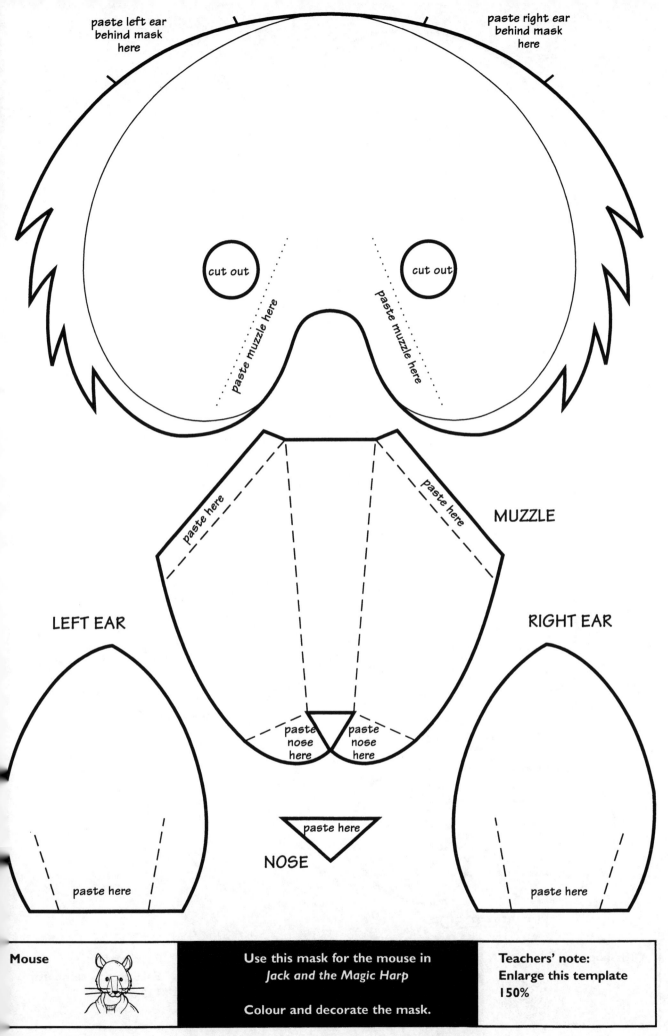

paste left ear behind mask here

paste right ear behind mask here

cut out

cut out

paste muzzle here

paste muzzle here

paste here

Paste here

MUZZLE

LEFT EAR

RIGHT EAR

paste nose here

paste nose here

paste here

NOSE

paste here

paste here

Mouse

Use this mask for the mouse in
Jack and the Magic Harp

Colour and decorate the mask.

Teachers' note:
Enlarge this template
150%

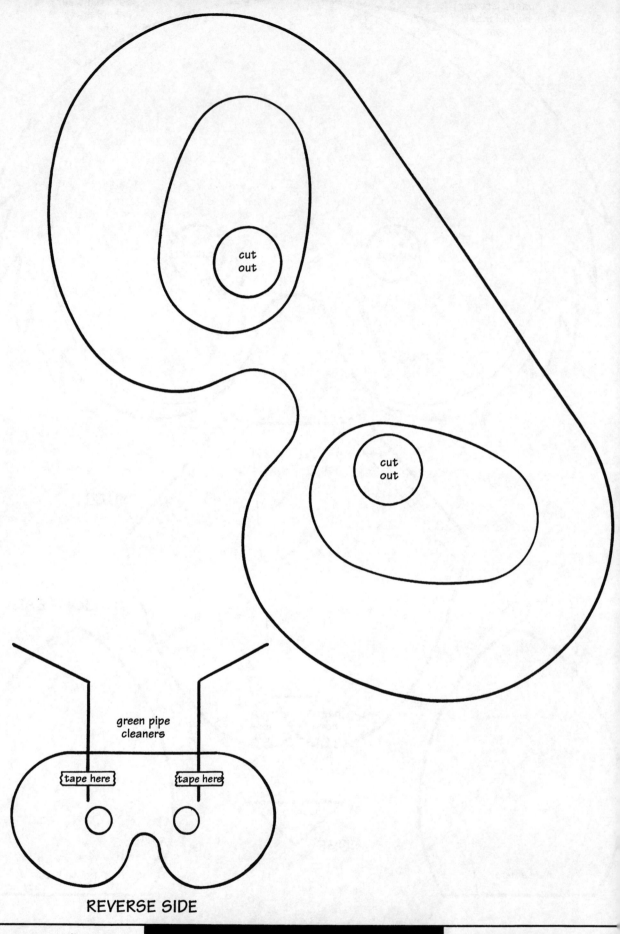

cut
out

cut
out

green pipe
cleaners

tape here   tape here

REVERSE SIDE

| Grasshopper | Use this mask for the grasshopper in *Jack and the Magic Harp*

Colour and decorate the mask. | Teachers' note:
Enlarge this template 150% |

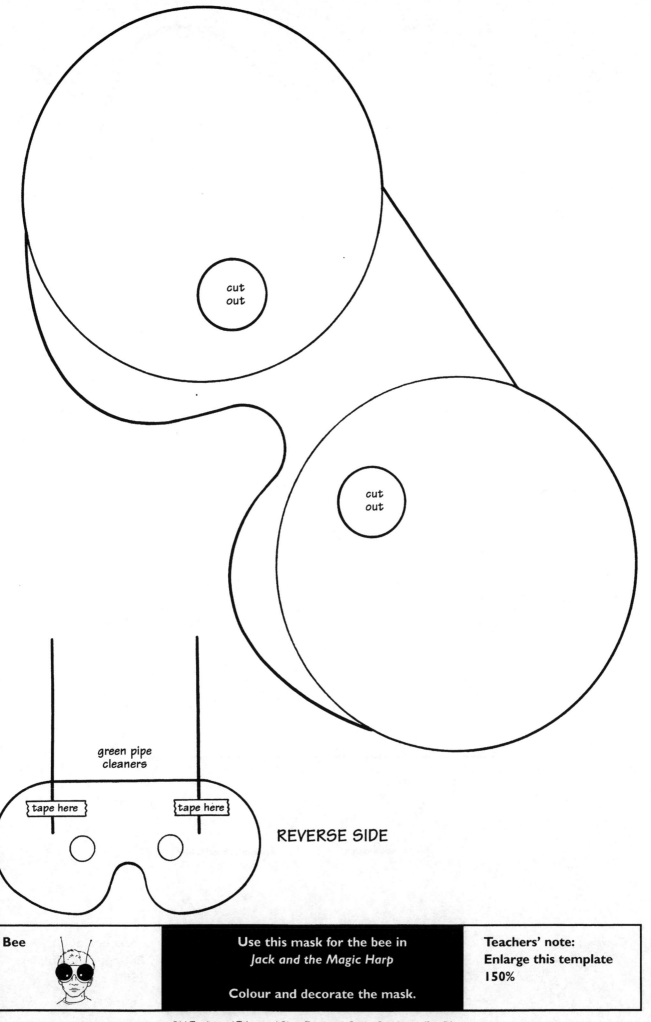

cut
out

cut
out

green pipe
cleaners

tape here   tape here

REVERSE SIDE

Bee

Use this mask for the bee in
Jack and the Magic Harp

Colour and decorate the mask.

Teachers' note:
Enlarge this template
150%

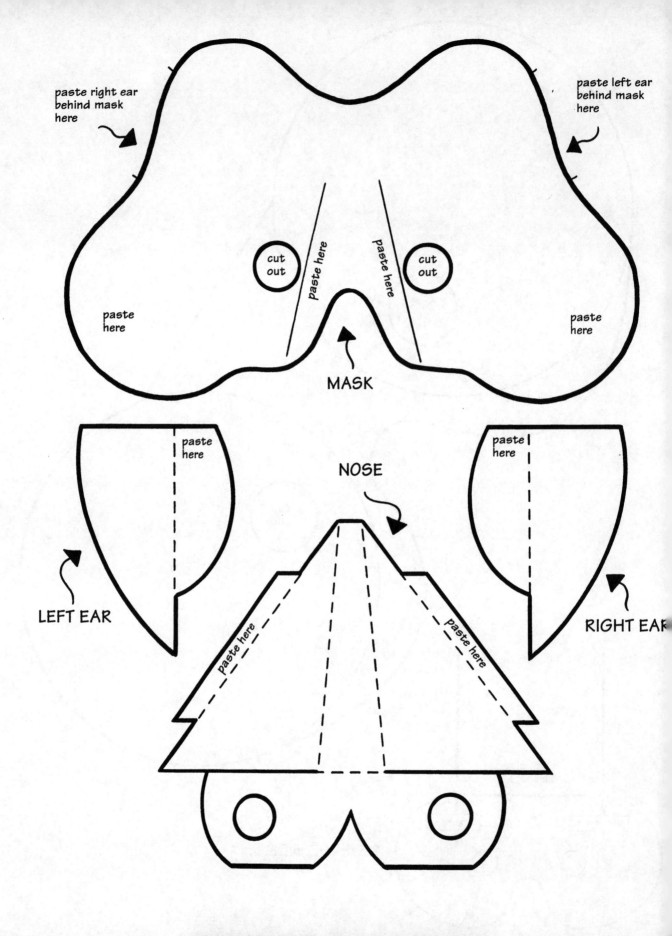

paste right ear behind mask here

paste left ear behind mask here

cut out

paste here

paste here

cut out

paste here

paste here

MASK

paste here

paste here

NOSE

LEFT EAR

RIGHT EAR

paste here

paste here

Cow

Use this mask for the cow in
Jack and the Magic Harp

Colour and decorate the mask.

Teachers' note:
Enlarge this template
150%

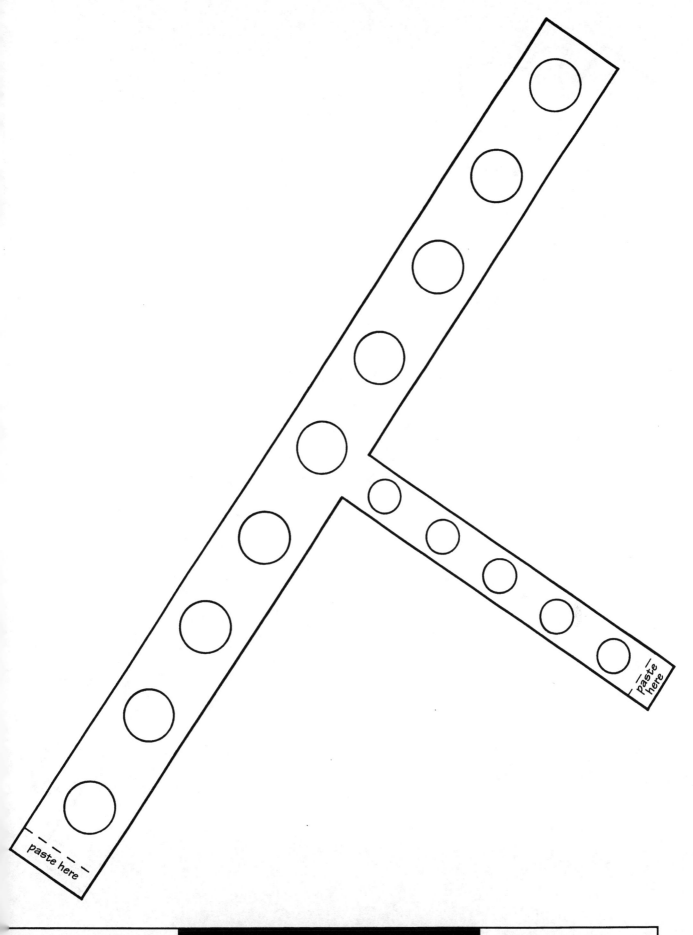

paste here

paste here

Soldier's hat

Use this template for the soldier's hat in *Jack and the Magic Harp*

Colour and decorate the template.

Teachers' note:
Enlarge this template 150%

paste here

Princess' crown

Use this template for the princess' crown in
Jack and the Magic Harp

Colour and decorate the template.

Teachers' note:
Enlarge this template
150%

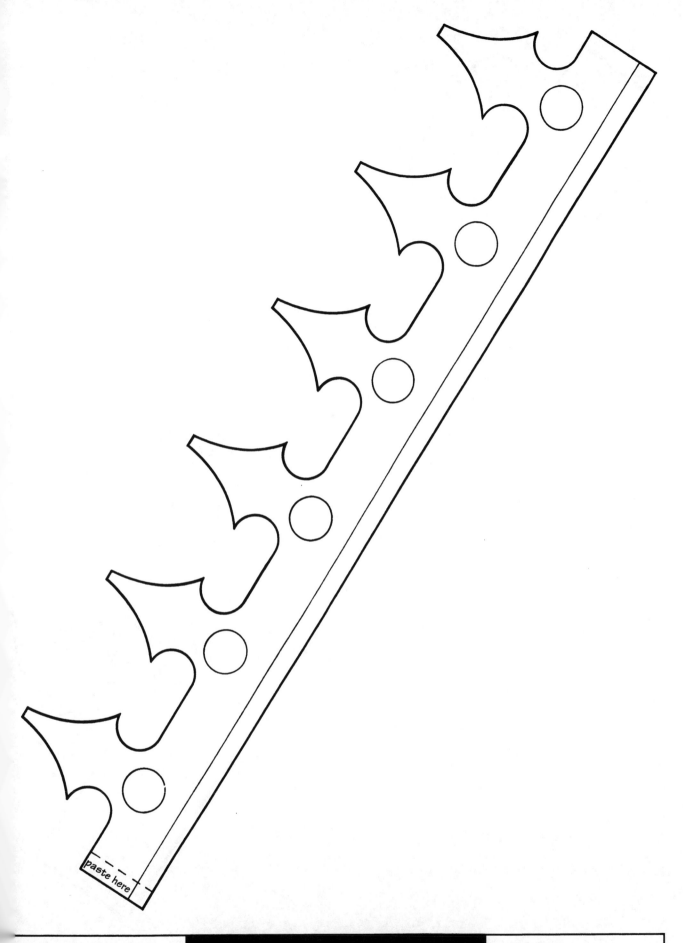

paste here

Queen's crown

Use this template for the queen's crown in
Snow White and the Seven Dwarfs

Colour and decorate the template.

Teachers' note:
Enlarge this template
150%

PM Traditional Tales and Plays Teachers' Guide Gold Level (Set D)

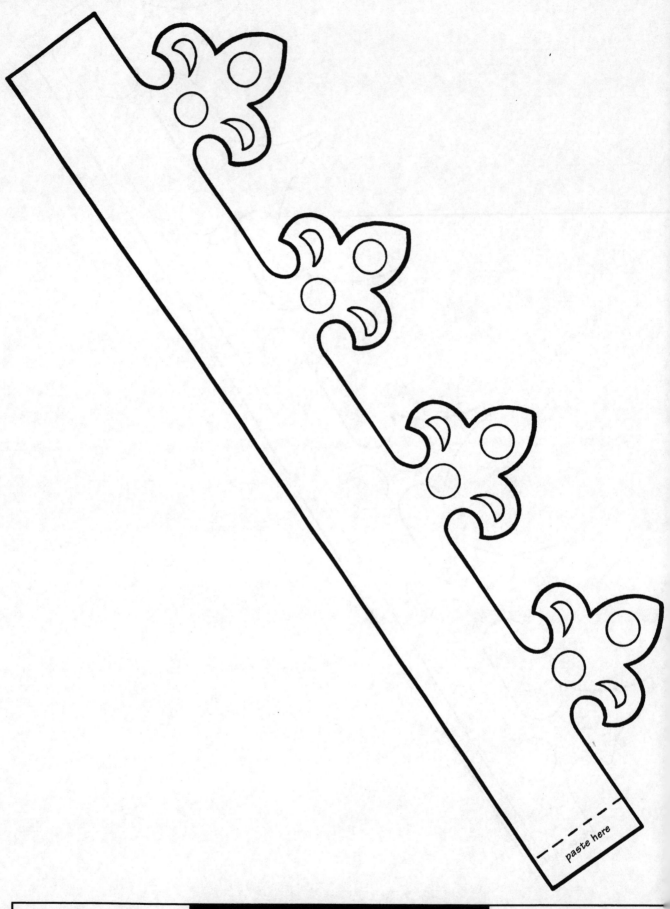

paste here

King's crown

Use this template for the king's crown in *Rumpelstiltskin*

Colour and decorate the template.

Teachers' note:
Enlarge this template
150%

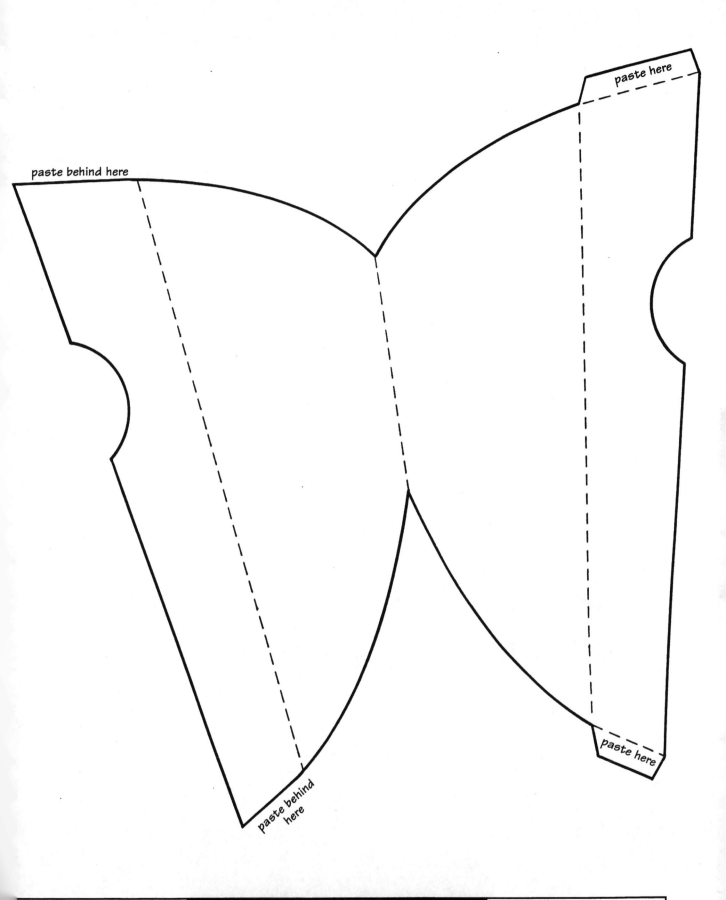

paste here

paste behind here

paste behind here

paste here

| Huntsman's/
Prince's
servants' hat | Use this template for the Huntsman's/Prince's
servants' hat in
Snow White and the Seven Dwarfs
Colour and decorate the template. | Teachers' note:
Enlarge this template
150% |

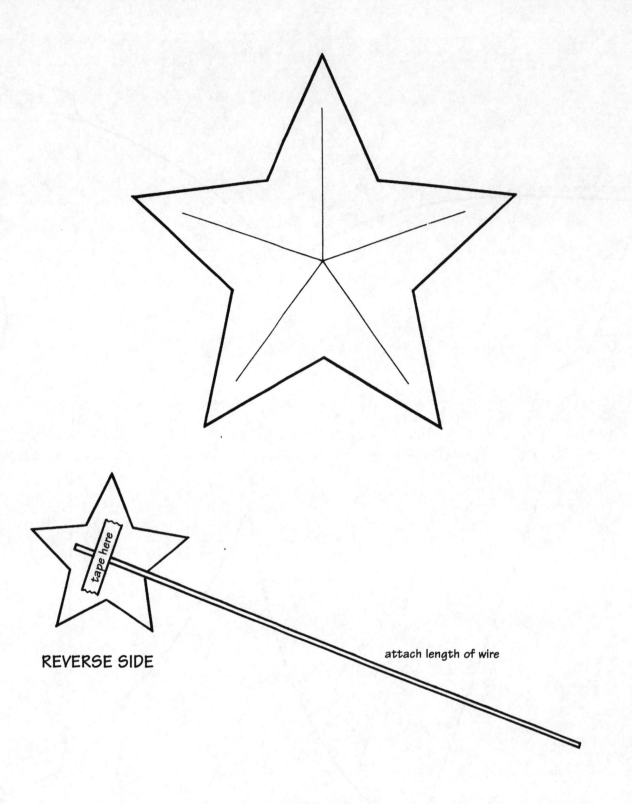

tape here

REVERSE SIDE

attach length of wire

Wand **Use this template for the wand in**
Cinderella

Colour and decorate the template.

**Teachers' note:
Enlarge this template
150%**

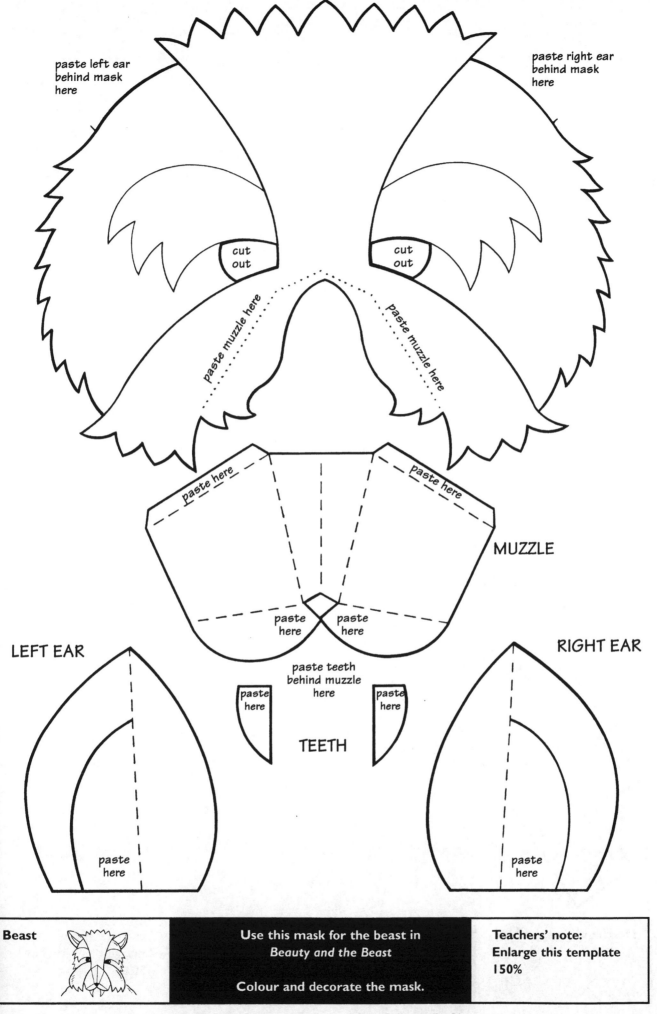

paste left ear behind mask here

paste right ear behind mask here

cut out

cut out

paste muzzle here

paste muzzle here

paste here

paste here

MUZZLE

paste here

paste here

LEFT EAR

RIGHT EAR

paste teeth behind muzzle here

paste here

paste here

TEETH

paste here

paste here

Beast

Use this mask for the beast in
Beauty and the Beast

Colour and decorate the mask.

Teachers' note:
Enlarge this template 150%

PM Traditional Tales and Plays Teachers' Guide Gold Level (Set D)

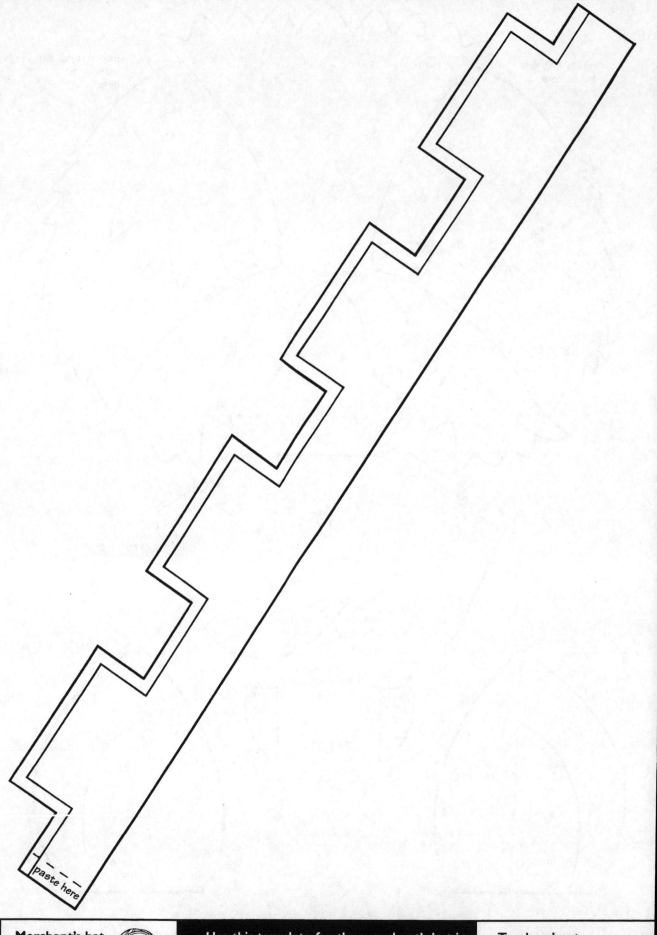

paste here

 Merchant's hat

Use this template for the merchant's hat in *Beauty and the Beast*

Colour and decorate the template.

Teachers' note:
Enlarge this template 150%

PM Traditional Tales and Plays Teachers' Guide Gold Level (Set D)